THE WRATH OF GRAPES

THE WRATH OF GRAPES
or
THE HANGOVER COMPANION

Andy Toper
Illustrated by Graham Round

SOUVENIR PRESS

First published 1996 by
Souvenir Press Ltd.,
43 Great Russell Street, London WC1B 3PA
and simultaneously in Canada

ISBN 0 285 63338 4

Typeset by Galleon Typesetting, Ipswich
Printed in Great Britain by The Bath Press, Bath

For
'The Directors'
Here's to the next one!

'He who eats a fine dinner and drinks too much over-night, wants a bottle of soda-water and a grill, perhaps, in the morning.'

W. M. Thackeray,
Maxims of Charles J. Yellowplush

CONTENTS

1   In the Drink   9
    The Painful History of Hangovers

2   One Over the Eight   21
    Understanding Your Hangover

3   The Complete Imbiber   34
    *or, How to Avoid a Hangover Without
    Becoming Teetotal*

4   The Morning After   47
    A Little of What Will do You Good

5   Hair of the Dog   73
    A Vade-mecum of Remedies

6   Three Sheets to the Wind   104
    The Wit and Wisdom of Drinking

    Bibliography   123

    Acknowledgements   126

ONE

IN THE DRINK
The Painful History of Hangovers

The first man to have a real humdinger of a hangover—or the first we know of—was probably Noah.
The Bible tells us in Genesis that 'Noah began to be
an husbandman, and he planted a vineyard. And he
drank of the wine, and was drunken.' Unless the
man who built the Ark was different from the rest of
us, he no doubt woke up the following morning with a thumping head, dry mouth and upset
stomach. He may even have been the first man to
vow '*Never* again!' before wondering how on earth he
could recover his equilibrium. His descendants—all
of us, that is, save those dedicated teetotallers—have
been wondering the same ever since.

Both the Greeks and the Romans were not slow
in following the old man's example (as an example
he was certainly exceptional, apparently surviving the

world's first recorded hangover to live to the grand old age of 950!). The two great ancient civilisations loved wine, women and song aplenty, and naturally paid the price for their overindulgence. The Greeks seem to have come up with the first idea for preventing hangovers. They apparently believed that amethysts could counter the heady fumes of wine and therefore studded their goblets with the precious stones.

When this idea didn't have the desired effect, the Greeks proposed that flagellation would release the blood tainted by alcohol and so clear the system. This remedy seems to have been no more successful, a pain in the head probably being preferable to a whipping for most people! One of the country's great chroniclers, Strabo (60 BC–AD 21) records that many of his fellow countrymen actually *prevented* themselves from getting drunk by mixing their wine with sea water which, naturally, made them sick! Strabo, who appears to have favoured this hangover preventative himself, could be said to have deserved his name which translates literally as 'squint-eyed'.

The Romans, who could certainly match the Greeks when it came to orgies of feasting and drinking, were the first people to make a study of the hangover. To Gaius Plinius Secundus (Pliny the

Pliny the Elder . . . the first recorder of hangover remedies.

Elder, AD 23–79), the soldier turned man-of-letters who produced 160 manuscript volumes during his lifetime, belongs the honour of being the first recorder of remedies. In one of his books he states that hangovers can be avoided by wearing a necklace of parsley when retiring to bed after a heavy drinking session; or cured the following morning by swallowing two raw owl's eggs in wine. Another cure he noted was swigging down a mixture of garlic and warm olive oil—the garlic to purify the blood and the oil to soothe the queasy stomach. While parsley necklaces have now rather gone out of favour as a curative, the raw egg, olive oil and garlic have all become staple ingredients in several recommended cures, as I shall reveal later.

It was the Romans, too, who came up with the concept of 'a hair of the dog'. According to custom, if anyone was bitten by a dog he would attempt to ward off the ill-effects by drinking a potion that contained some *burnt* hairs of the offending canine. From this came the idea of countering overindulgence in wine, spirits or beer with more of the same. Medically speaking, to add alcohol to a body already suffering from an excess might be said to do it no good at all. Yet as anyone who has tried it knows, it *does* induce a feeling of well-being—albeit temporary in some cases!

In England, where the same principle was employed in treating the bite of a mad dog by putting some of the animal's hairs *onto the wound*, the term 'hair of the dog' is known to have been in use as early as 1546. It turned up then in a work of John Heywood, the epigrammatist and playwright, best known for his poem *The Spider and the Flie*, who wrote:

> I pray thee let me and my fellows have
> A Haire of the dog that bit us last night.

The Middle Ages are particularly rich in stories of supposed cures for the morning after. In an age when kings and noblemen indulged their lusts and their thirsts unchecked by conventions, any number of charlatans offered the most preposterous remedies to those who would buy them. Eye of newt and limb of toad were just two of the less revolting ingredients. After prescribing which, these men no doubt made off as quickly as they could before their hungover victims *really* recovered! A few of the remedies, however, actually seem to have worked—including one, documented in Britain in the sixteenth century, which prescribed a mixture of raw eels and bitter almonds ground into a paste and eaten with hunks of bread. Even then, people were beginning to appreciate that what they ate both before and after a drinking session could be important to their subsequent state of health—for more of which see Chapter 3 *et seq*.

Perhaps even more unappetising was a remedy used in the American Wild West where men were men, women were women and the whiskey was often bad. The frontiersman who wanted to soothe his aching head after a night in the saloon was told to make a drink of hot water and *jackrabbit droppings*! These pellets had to be dried before they were used and then allowed to dissolve in the hot water for at least an hour. During this time, the mixture apparently turned a disgusting brown colour, which probably made the thought of drinking it more appalling than the hangover.

Curiously, although we use the word 'hangover' to describe the multitude of symptoms that leave us the worse for wear on the morning after, the term itself has only been in use this century. It has been suggested that it was coined in America, but there is nothing to substantiate this, and the earliest reference

The hangover cure of the Wild West.

actually appears in a comic volume published in England in 1904, entitled *The Foolish Directory*. This book, ostensibly compiled by one 'G. Wurdz', mentions the term in the entry for **Brain**. I quote: 'The Brain is usually occupied by the Intellect Brothers—Thoughts and Ideas—as an Intelligence Office, but sometimes sub-let to Jag. Hang-Over & Co.'

To be fair, it may well be true that the use of the word 'hangover' to describe the well-known feeling of malaise first became commonplace in America, and it can certainly be found in the books of Will Irwin, a writer of picaresque tales around the years of the First World War. This great humorist, war correspondent and journalist, who was also one of the liveliest members of the Dutch Treat Club in New York, penned these lines in *The Red Button* (1912): 'This was the first time in his life that Tommy North had ever admitted a "hangover".' In view of the malady's long history, there is something rather amusing about those quotation marks!

What is beyond doubt is that by 1918 the expression had found its way into American dictionaries—probably reinforced by the campaigns of the temperance societies and the advent of Prohibition, of which more later—where it was defined as 'a headache, nausea, etc. occurring as an after effect of drinking much alcoholic liquor'. English dictionaries followed suit two years later.

A much older term, which seems to have fallen into disuse in its original form but has taken on a whole new meaning in a shortened version, is 'crapulent', an adjective which means 'a hangover caused by excessive drinking', according to my *Chambers Twentieth Century Dictionary*. However, all over the world, the ever ingenious drinking classes have come up with their own terminology for the universal hangover, of which the following are just a few of my favourites:

- *La Gueule de bois* or *La GDB*—from France, which translates as 'a mouth of wood'.

- *Katzenjammer*—the German term, meaning 'a wailing of cats'.

- *Kater*—from Holland, which also means 'noisy cats'.

- *Resaca*—the Spanish and Portuguese word to indicate 'a surge'.

- *Malessere dopo una sbornia*—used by the Italians for 'a sickness after a booze-up' (alternatively, some Italians prefer *Stonato*, or 'out of tune').

- *Jeg har tommermen*—a wonderfully explicit Norwegian phrase meaning 'carpenters in the head'.

- *Tommermaend*—a variation from Denmark which translates as 'carpentered'.

- *Hont i hare*—perhaps the best term of all from neighbouring Sweden, meaning 'a pain in the roots of the hair'.

There is total agreement when it comes to the major cause and effect of hangovers. They are caused primarily by little chemical elements known as congeneric substances or congeners, which provide the taste, aroma and colour to alcoholic drinks. The effect is dehydration, headache and indigestion. Just what the congeners are, how they operate when they get into the bloodstream, and the means of coping with their machinations will be discussed later.

Research into the hangover, begun by the Romans all those centuries ago, has subsequently exercised the minds of quite a number of people, from pollsters to researchers, not to mention the poor old hungover 'man in the street'. In Australia, for example, just a few years ago, a survey to find the worst sufferers put the drinkers of Western Australia at the top of the poll, with 38 per cent of those questioned suffering at least one per week. The folk of Queensland, whether by abstinence or more abstemious habits, finished at the bottom with less than 10 per cent.

In England, in 1992, *Which?* magazine, the journal of the Consumers' Association, conducted a survey of pick-me-up remedies. The team of investigators covered a variety of proprietary brands as well as looking into their readers' own suggestions. They concluded that there was *no* ideal cure, although some of the remedies varied from 'the good to the disastrous'. Also in England, the first hangover clinic was recently opened, offering the afflicted a sauna, a short treatment with pure oxygen and a cocktail of fruit and sugar including the vitamins B1, B6 and C, plus garden mint. The clinic apparently topped off its service with the offer of a massage and a strong cup of tea.

No matter how many times a hangover victim holds his head in his hands in the grey light of morning and mutters, 'Never, *never* again!' the evidence suggests that such resolutions last for most of us until temptation rears its flavoursome head or, more likely, opening time. It was Shakespeare, I think, who said (doubtless with the benefit of experience), 'Oh God, that men should put an enemy in their mouths to steal away their brains.'

I can't guarantee to put that enemy to flight in these pages—but I can make you aware of how to fight the battle and get the upper hand. Until the next time, at least . . .

TWO

ONE OVER THE EIGHT
Understanding Your Hangover

Drinking alcohol affects people in very different ways, which is probably why, after all these years, we are still not sure exactly *how* hangovers occur, nor have we found the perfect remedy. We have all met the poor soul who descends into sentimental drivel, or have tried to avoid the aggressive bully. For some people, a single drink can be the only step required to cause a hangover, while others tipple away all night long with barely a twinge of pain or conscience the following morning.

Take, for example, Bobby Acland of the Black Raven pub in Bishopsgate, London, who holds the *Guinness Book of Records* entry for consuming three bottles of champagne a day (that's over a thousand bottles per annum) and claims never to have had a hangover, only a renewed sense of anticipation every morning for more bubbly. Even his achievement, however, pales in comparison with the boozing skills of one of our former Prime Ministers, William Pitt the Younger. In a single year around the beginning of the nineteenth century he is said to have put away 574 bottles of claret, 854 bottles of Madeira and 2,410 bottles of port . . . and still carried out his duties in the House of Commons. Some might argue that, on the keen performances of certain contemporary politicians, what's changed?

The Welsh poet Dylan Thomas also acquired a legendary reputation for being able to drink most of his friends and acquaintances under the table and rarely complained of being under the weather the next day. He, too, has a place in the annals of drink, albeit a tragic one, for his last words are said to have been, 'I've had 18 straight whiskies—I think that's the record.'

Drinking, however, should not be about abusing the mind and body but rather, as Cicero put it, for 'the replenishment of our strength, not for our sorrow', and this book is certainly not intended for those of a self-destructive disposition. It is about what makes us drunk, what causes hangovers, and how to tackle the inevitable consequences. The late Sir Kingsley Amis, a man dedicated to the arts of writing and drinking (a few sour critics have argued that they should be placed in reverse order), had this to say on the matter: 'Like the search for god, with which it has other things in common, the search for the infallible and instantaneous hangover cure will never be done.'

Despite his cynicism, the redoubtable Sir Kingsley nevertheless admitted that there is always something new to say on the subject of drinking and that, over the years, a good many truths about it have been established. Curiously, they are the sort of truths that in certain cases the anti-alcohol lobby would prob-ably rather not hear. Take these examples:

- Alcohol is *not* a stimulant, it is a sedative.
- Pure alcohol does *not* produce fat—which is a weight off your stomach.
- Alcohol will *not* warm the body—its actual effect is the opposite.
- Alcohol is *not* good for heat exhaustion—quite the reverse.
- Mixing drinks is *not* what makes you drunk—it's the alcohol content in each that is to blame.

One of these statements may require a little elaboration. The feeling of warmth from a snifter of whisky or brandy is actually caused by the heart pumping some warm blood to the cells at the periphery of the body. So, if the conditions are cold, the result is just the opposite of what you *actually* want: you are warm on the surface but cold inside.

So, if we now have some idea of what alcohol doesn't do, what *does* it do?

According to the best estimates of the medical profession, the human body has 96,000 kilometres (that's almost 52,000 miles) of blood vessels, some of which are so thin that the blood corpuscles can only pass along them in single file. It is the impurities in the alcohol we guzzle into our bloodstream which most authorities now agree are the main cause of hangovers. These are the congeners, which the *Oxford English Dictionary* defines as 'a chemical by-product in the making of whisky, etc., which gives the drink a distinctive character'. They occur naturally in the course of fermentation, giving alcoholic drinks their individual taste, colour and clarity. The congeners consist of chemicals such as fusel oils, organic acids, aldehydes and other toxins and it is these sneaky little villains, occurring in large enough numbers, that get to work in the stomach and brain to cause hangovers. But that is only part of the story.

It may come as a surprise to learn that all of us—drinker and strict teetotaller alike—have *some* alcohol in our bloodstreams *all the time*. The amount can be as little as .003 per cent, but it is *always* present as a result of the action of the gastric juices on the sugars and starches we eat. Alcohol is therefore a necessity in the bloodstream and will not damage any of the vital organs—the heart, liver, kidneys, brain, stomach or nervous system—*unless* the normal level is exceeded by prolonged and heavy drinking.

During the course of an average drinking session, when the percentage of alcohol in the bloodstream rises to .1, inhibitions are freed; at .2 per cent muscle control is affected; and by .4 incoherence has just about taken over. Any further alcohol then can seriously endanger the drinker's life. (The highest recorded figure of alcohol in the bloodstream was discovered by a Liverpool pathologist in May 1979, when he was examining the body of a Merseyside car worker, Samuel Riley. The dead man had a level of 1220 mg. per 100 ml. of blood.)

So, when we raise a glass of spirit and swallow it

with a hearty 'Cheers!' what happens? The effect is actually remarkably quick, because alcohol behaves unlike anything else we imbibe. It goes straight to the stomach and thence directly into the bloodstream, without being affected chemically by any of the digestive juices. The walls of the stomach soak up about one-third of the pure alcohol in the drink, with the remaining two-thirds being absorbed into the intestinal walls.

As soon as the alcohol hits the bloodstream, it begins to work. The reason for this is that, among its many qualities, it is a narcotic as well as a mild anaesthetic.

Firstly, alcohol has the narcotic effect of relaxing the walls of our blood vessels, which gets the heart beating faster and causes the skin temperature to rise. That's where the talk about the 'warm glow' of the first drink originates.

Secondly, alcohol has a unique anaesthetic quality when it floods into the capillaries of the brain. Here it quite literally gives our brain cells a shot of ether in the form of ethanol (the main type of alcohol in drinks), which is actually quite closely allied to alcohol in medical terms. It shuts down the part of our brain that doctors refer to as the 'inhibitory centre' and forces the nerve cells to adapt to the new situation. (This, incidentally, was the reason why alcohol was used so frequently by earlier generations of doctors when carrying out surgery.)

What this medical jargon actually means is those little pricks (no pun intended) of conscience which control the way we behave. As everyone who has ever taken a drop knows, alcohol brings on a state of euphoria in which worries seem to disappear, our sense of responsibility whispers goodbye, and all our faults are as nothing. It gives us a 'lift', makes us 'high', and we feel **GREAT**!

But our insidious friend alcohol does not stop at putting the brain into neutral. It weaves its way around the whole of the body, anaesthetising the various other motor centres. That is when speech can become slurred, knees begin to wobble, and stupor is not far behind if we continue to hoover up every drink in sight.

According to the received wisdom of the medical profession, many of whose members are not averse to practising what they preach, the average body can cope with $\frac{1}{200}$ of an ounce of alcohol per minute, or about one ounce of 80 per cent proof spirit per hour. To exceed this amount by three times over the same

Cheers....

Our insidious friend alcohol . . .

period can make the old expression 'paralysed with drink' come true—*literally*. For what happens is that the drinker's organs actually do become paralysed.

Of course, the impact of alcohol varies from drinker to drinker, with a newcomer to spirits almost certainly experiencing that sense of euphoria some time before the regular imbiber. Genetics and size are also believed to be contributory factors. The tippler whose parents have been drinkers may well have inherited a greater tolerance than someone from a teetotal background; while the bigger a person's body, the better equipped he is to cope with a large intake of alcohol.

Another side-effect of alcohol that *does* affect us all is that it makes us go to the loo more often. This has nothing to do with whether we are drinking beer or spirits. The reason is simply that alcohol is a diuretic. Normally, when the brain is unimpaired by drink, it conducts through the body the flow of an important and beneficial hormone known as an antidiuretic, which stops the body from getting rid of useful fluids. Without it, our lives would be one non-stop pee.

Hence, the more alcohol you consume, the less antidiuretic is in circulation. So even though you may be drinking a lot of fluid, your body is just as quickly crying out to get rid of it. A natural consequence is that the balance of water in the body's cells and tissues is altered, causing dehydration. The brain swells when the blood vessels leading to the cerebral tissues dilate, raising the blood pressure, and the result is a throbbing headache.

To those who really know about hangovers, there is no getting away from the impact of the congeners which give booze its look and aroma, for, contrary to what your taste buds may tell you, alcohol itself has *no* taste. Produced during the fermentation and maturing process, there are about a hundred different types—that have so far been counted, I hasten to add.

Evidence suggests that the richer, darker drinks like whisky, bourbon, brandy, dark rum, port, sherry, vermouth and red wine contain a lot more congeners than the paler varieties such as vodka, gin, Bacardi and white wine. And popular lore has it that the darker the colour of the drink, the worse the hangover it generates—which is what has given these chemicals such a black label. True it may well be but, conversely, there is no guarantee that by drinking only the lighter spirits you can avoid a hangover!

Undoubtedly there are also other factors which contribute to the discomfort of a hangover. Alcohol stimulates the manufacture of insulin in the body, which in turn reduces the levels of blood sugar. A consequence of this is a feeling of drowsiness and hunger (to the eternal gratitude of every late night curry house or fish and chip shop). Alcohol also upsets the body's metabolism and this causes a rise in acidity. Because all the cells in the body are dehydrated, the acid–base metabolism is altered and the result is the sensation of sickness and depression.

While our bodies are hard at work breaking down the alcohol slurped into it, some toxic chemicals are being produced. In large amounts, of course, they could be poisonous, though in the average night of drinking the amount is likely to be unpleasant rather than serious. Particularly significant among these toxins is methanol, a type of alcohol found as a congener in most spirits. It is metabolised in exactly the same way as ethanol, but along the way produces some distasteful chemicals.

The fact is that our bodies won't get to work on the methanol until most of the ethanol has been broken down, and the chances are that the toxins produced by the methanol won't begin to form until hours after you have started drinking, probably not until you wake up the next morning. That is what contributes the upset stomach to the hangover. Interestingly, not everyone metabolises the methanol in their system at the same rate, which is why some doctors believe that certain people suffer less than others on the morning after.

For most men and women, drinking sooner or later lulls them into the land of nod. Some—you happy band!—enjoy a good night's sleep and wake none the worse. For others, the chances are they will wake up far too early and find it difficult to get back to sleep again. Even those short interludes of dreaming sleep—known as REM or Rapid Eye Movement sleep—which are thought to be an important factor in how refreshed a person feels on waking the next day, can be impaired by alcohol. Under these circumstances, the fabled arms of Morpheus may be as heartily cursed by a sleepless mind as the King's Arms where all the trouble began.

The explanation of this problem is that under the sedative effects of alcohol, the body compensates by making the nervous system more sensitive than normal. And when the high spirits—both literally and figuratively—have subsided, the nervous system is left in overdrive, generating a feeling of restlessness. This is also the reason why noises can seem louder and lights much brighter during a hangover.

Even though the hangover (by any other name) has been with us since Noah's time—and intensified by an Arab who invented the distillation process to manufacture what he called *al-kuhl*—there is still much about it that is submerged in mystery. As one stalwart enquirer, as keen to be able to get to the bottom of the problem as to the bottom of his glass without repercussions, put it recently, 'The hangover is a malady without a country.'

Certainly, research into man's oldest malady has not been undertaken by scientists on the scale its prevalence surely deserves; nor given greater regard by the medical profession who mostly see it as something for which the victim has only himself to blame. Yet the hangover remains a universal problem that has to be faced by most people at one time or other in their lives.

What better time than now, ladies and gentlemen, *if you please*!

THREE

THE COMPLETE IMBIBER

Or, How to Avoid a Hangover Without Becoming Teetotal

So you want to avoid being hungover? To wake up without your head thumping, your mouth parched, breath like a jockey's underpants, and your stomach complaining at every movement? This whole sensation has been very aptly described, with what sounds like the knowledge of personal experience, by writer Raymond Carver as 'being about one step to the left and five feet above one's own physical body'.

The only certain way to avoid man's oldest affliction is, of course, not to drink at all—and this was very much part of the message of the temperance societies which sprang up on both sides of the Atlantic in the last quarter of the nineteenth century. These groups of sobersides—among the most powerful being the Women's Christian Temperance Union, founded in 1874, and the American Anti-Saloon League twenty years later, in 1893—were dedicated to inducing people to abstain from alcoholic beverages of every kind.

One of the largest of these organisations, based in New York, is credited with inspiring the word *teetotal* by instructing its members to place a large capital 'T' after their signatures to indicate to all the world their total abstinence from the demon drink. Legend has it that some bar-room wags soon began referring to them as the 'T-totals' and so the label stuck. The high-point of the campaign by the groups—which undoubtedly influenced the passage of many liquor laws—was the era of Federal Prohibition between 1920 and 1933.

Even under the toughest restrictions, however, keen drinkers will always find a way to hang one on. Throughout the whole thirteen-year period, right under the unsullied noses of the New York anti-hooch brigade, drinking dens were constantly being opened. In one year alone their number actually *doubled*. And despite all the legislation forbidding the manufacture and transportation of booze, the fact never seems to have quite got through to the officials at the US Department of Agriculture: throughout this time they continued to distribute to anyone who asked a leaflet describing precisely how to extract alcohol from apples, bananas, pumpkins and similar fermentable fruits!

If we are not going to follow the advice of the teetotallers, we need to take a sober look at the alternatives.

Centuries of bitter (and wine and spirits) experience have proved beyond all doubt that to booze it up, whether deliberately or unintentionally, on an empty stomach is a recipe for disaster. It is absolutely essential to line the stomach, because food prevents the alcohol from being immediately absorbed into the bloodstream, with all that ensues. Our stomachs do this by closing off the pyloric valve, the passageway to the intestines, and forcing the drink through the slower route via the stomach walls.

A full stomach is also regarded as a good psychological barrier and may well help a drinker to consume less and protect the inner man from the onslaught of those dreaded congeners. As a general rule, proteins are said to be better at aiding the body's processes of absorption than carbohydrates.

As a matter of fact, alcohol itself can be looked

upon as food—albeit a special kind—which consists of a mixture of carbohydrates and water. An
ounce of whisky, for example, liberates 75 calories of
energy or the equivalent of four and a half teaspoonfuls of sugar. So, taken in an emergency, a shot can
provide a useful boost of energy. However, these
calories *can't* be stored in the body; *can't* repair body
tissues (only protein does that) and *can't* add to our
fuel reserves by producing fats. They are very much
in short-time occupation. None the less, alcohol
energy *can* be useful, and the trick is for *you* to use
the energy and not to let the energy use you.

It is worth bearing in mind that your stomach is
well aware of the difference between diluted and
undiluted spirits. There is no pulling the wool over
a tummy—or woolly is how you will feel later.
Undiluted drink takes longer to be absorbed because
the stronger proof activates the stomach lining into
producing a mucus to protect itself, at the same time
as closing off the pyloric valve. Always beware of the
false sense of security a diluted drink may give—the
effect is only being delayed!

History reveals that over the centuries people all
over the world have prepared their stomachs against
the ravages of alcohol in a variety of ways—right back

to the time of those incorrigible Romans. They, for example, discovered that the humble cabbage had special preventative powers, and either swallowed cabbage seeds before a night at the orgy or, alternatively, consumed a plate of boiled cabbage before settling down for the night. Whether they knew it or not, the reason *why* cabbage is such a help is because it is a chelator: a substance which amalgamates with other elements and carries them out of the body.

The Russians had similar faith in the cucumber. A mixture of the juice squeezed from an unpeeled cucumber heavily salted (at least two teaspoonfuls) was said to be a great favourite with the Cossacks who were notorious for their bravery and bingeing. Whether they were brave enough to face the hangover remedy of their neighbours in Outer Mongolia is not known. This consisted of the juice of tomatoes drunk with a *pickled sheep's eye*!

The Welsh had an equally stomach-turning preventative against getting drunk. The main ingredient was the roasted lungs of a pig. If eaten for breakfast, the 'recipe' promised, with nothing else passing the lips all day, it would be impossible to become drunk, no matter how much alcohol was consumed that night.

In Spain it has long been the custom for men and women to take a glass of virgin olive oil before attending any celebration where they may be expected to down the odd gallon or two of wine. Olive oil is said to protect the stomach lining and to slow down the absorption of alcohol. In Ireland, the one essential preliminary to a *ceile* is a big plate of mashed potatoes mixed with slices of spring onion. Another favourite with the Irish is a mixture of lamb stew and potatoes served between two slices of bread and referred to, appropriately, as a 'battle burger'!

The Americans also favour a big, solid meal, the next best thing being a cup of broth or a glass of milk. In Britain a meal of pickled herrings has a reputation for preventing drunkenness. The reason is that these particular fish are so oily that they neutralise the effect of alcohol as soon as they hit the stomach. The same thing is claimed for sardines eaten on a piece of well-buttered toast.

Charcoal is another preventative that has been around since the Middle Ages, when drinkers first discovered its ability to absorb a large intake of the hard stuff. Some Victorian chimneysweeps, with their easy access to charcoal—and soot, which apparently worked just as well—made quite a bit on the side by

The essential preliminary to an Irish ceile . . .

selling portions to the gentry, which had to be taken in a glass of warm milk before a night on the town. Today, gritty little charcoal tablets are available from chemists for the same purpose, and I am told their effectiveness is enhanced by a tablespoon of olive oil.

The most extraordinary stomach-lining dish I have ever come across, however, was reported in the Brisbane *Courier-Mail* in 1991. It is more like a four-course meal than an attempt to head off a hangover and was, apparently, recommended by a doctor who was 'a world-famous authority on hangovers'—although the columnist who mentioned this veritable feast chose not to identify the potential saviour of the hard-drinking classes. 'Eat a bowl of milk and cornflakes (packed with vitamin B),' the doctor said, 'and next a whole orange (for its vitamin C). Follow this with a plate of potatoes, well salted and mashed with butter, and a glass of full-cream milk.' The columnist nick-named the doctor's preventative an 'Aussie Belly-Buster'—and who would disagree!

One thing to avoid in the battle against the hang-over is heavy smoking. The reason for this is pretty obvious: cigarettes and cigars make you want to drink more. As we know, alcohol makes the veins and arteries of the body expand—the medical term for this is a vasodilator—while the nicotine in a cigarette or a big Havana is a vasocontractor and constricts them. The effect of these two working against each other can be another factor in condemning you to a morning of retribution.

Experience plays an important part in avoiding a hangover. Even an occasional drinker soon learns which drinks he or she is more suited to. White wine, for instance, has become a favourite with lots of people who are probably unaware that their choice is a sound one because there are fewer of those sneaky little undercover agents, the congeners, in the drink. As a further precaution, the longer the drinking continues, top up white wine with still water or alternate with a glass of Vichy or Perrier water. This not only quenches the thirst but corrects acidity and freshens the palate. It takes time—and perhaps a little painful experience—to discover which congeners affect you most harshly, and then to learn to treat them with respect.

A drinker's capacity can also vary from time to time according to his or her physical and emotional condition. The death of someone close, the break-up of a marriage or an affair, can have a profound effect on a person's state of mind. And while a single drink may well be a relaxer under such circumstances, experience shows that more can influence even a regular drinker to a much greater extent than he might expect. As the American psychologist Dr Donald Williams wrote sagely on this topic a few years ago, 'Don't expect liquor to compensate—the label on the bottle makes no such promise.'

At the bottom line (and not on the bottle) drinking alcohol should be regarded as complementary to the pleasant art of living well and should never be used as a substitute for anything in either private or public life. It is only a means, never an end in itself.

If you must have a drink before going out for the evening to dinner or a party—and it's a perfectly understandable human trait to want to bolster your confidence a bit before meeting other people—then the general consensus of opinion is that a shot of iced vodka and some fresh caviar may be the best prelude—*if* you can afford it! The reason for this is that the vodka is free of congeners and, as a general rule, cold drinks work more slowly on the system than those at room temperature. Caviar, apart from being delicious, is also rich in proteins.

Another little tip. Never forget that fizzy alcoholic drinks such as champagne and the new breed of designer fruit tipples like Two Dogs, Hooper's Hooch and Piranha, are absorbed into the bloodstream much faster than the still varieties. That is because of the boost they are given by the carbon dioxide.

If there is a ready supply of food to hand in the pub or at a party, then don't be backward in coming forward for a regular nibble, as this will help slow down the rate at which the alcohol gets into your system. Plain almonds are especially good as they will delay and diminish the effects of too much alcohol, but beware of anything salted as this will only make you more thirsty and can wreck the best of intentions!

Besides the calories in alcohol which I mentioned earlier, many drinks have a food value of their own, like wine (with its vitamins) and beer (with its cereal carbohydrates), not forgetting all the drinks made with fruit juice. This is something to remember, especially when you are in the company of drinkers you know have a bigger capacity than your own.

Although mixing too many different kinds of drinks can have its dangers, it has been suggested that drinking one non-alcoholic drink for every alcoholic one enables you to opt for anything on offer—within reason. What actually matters is the *amount* of spirits consumed within a given period, not just the way it has been distilled or any fancy label it may carry.

Finally, no matter how much you have drunk during the evening or how confident you may feel that you have done everything to avoid the grim reality of a hangover next morning, there are still a few do's and don'ts to observe before surrendering to your urge to fall asleep.

Don't drink black coffee. It's an old wives' tale (or maybe a mother-in-law's) that a cup of strong black coffee is an antidote to alcohol. It isn't. Coffee keeps you awake, lengthens your evening and increases your input. The caffeine in it is more likely to keep you on the go and unaware of the impairment to your other faculties. If you want something warm, then hot chocolate is a viable alternative. The most famous recipe is one by Anthelme Brillat-Savarin, the legendary eighteenth-century French gastronome, who confided to his friends that the only sure way to prevent a hangover was to drink before going to bed 'a good pint of chocolate mixed with amber in the proportion of from sixty to seventy grains to the pound.'

Do drink a pint of water. The body needs lots of fluid to counter the diuretic effect of the alcohol you have been so happily imbibing. The water will not reduce the level of alcohol in the system, but it will help the liver and kidneys to cope with the invading hordes of congeners. So even if you hold the conviction that *aqua pura* is only really fit for fish to swim in, be brave and swallow for your head's sake! (I am reliably informed that a mixture of lime juice and water or a good old pinta milka may do as well.)

If you are still *compos mentis* enough to remember before turning in, a tablet of paracetamol (easier on the stomach than aspirin and better at dealing with a headache) or a seltzer powder—Alka or Bromo— can improve your insurance policy. There are a lot of people who swear that the 'tablet and water' routine before shut-eye definitely lessens the effect of a hangover.

But if there is one hard and fast rule about avoiding the hangover then it is this. Discover as soon as you can (trial and error are probably the only certain way) how much alcohol you can take with enjoyment and the amount you need for that buzz of well-being. Then drink *that* much—and no more. The decision and the price you may pay the following day are yours *alone*.

FOUR

THE MORNING AFTER
A Little of What Will do You Good

OK, so you've got a hangover. Despite everything—your good intentions, pre-drinking preparations, and even your determination *not* to have 'just one more' ('one for the road' is no longer politically correct, I'm told)—you're awake and feeling like death warmed up. Or, to put it gently—and everything has to be put *gently* at this stage—you've got a headache, an upset stomach, a mixed bag of feelings of nausea, tiredness and depression, and find yourself the reluctant owner of a thirst you could photograph. You may even have a touch of the shakes if things are really bad.

The thirst, in fact, is probably the major part of the problem because, according to medical specialists and doctors alike, most hangovers are triggered by dehydration. This was certainly the unshakeable belief of Sir Kingsley Amis who admitted, 'I always keep

several bottles of mineral water beside my bed—
always, so I don't have to do any special remember-
ing—and can start working on my dehydration as
soon as I wake up.'

Of course, just about everyone you meet has a
suggestion for curing a hangover. Some of them are
old folk remedies, others bar-made, and the rest use
branded pharmaceutical products. There is even the
odd one or two based on pure accident. A favourite
story of mine was told me by George Farrow, a
former Army officer who served in Malaysia in the
Sixties and enjoyed the odd *stingah* or four. One
morning, nursing what he described as 'the mother
and father of hangovers', George was faced with a
drive from Ipoh to the Cameron Highlands, an
ascent of some 6,000 feet. It was all he could do to
keep his hands on the wheel as he drove the 38 miles
up a tortuous mountain road through the jungle. But
something very curious happened as he was motor-
ing along.

'The higher I climbed,' George recalled, 'the more
my hangover disappeared. By the time I reached the
Cameron Highlands my head was completely clear
and my stomach no longer felt queasy. I was ready for
lunch and even a few more drinks—the thought of

which would have made me throw up earlier.'

George tucked into his meal and liquid refreshment with renewed relish, and later set off back to Ipoh. 'I don't suppose I'd gone more than a few miles downhill before a strange sensation crept over me. I felt my hangover coming back! By the time I reached the main road a "hair of the dog" was imperative and I stopped at the nearest bar to have "two for one"!'

The simple explanation of this phemonenon might be that climbing a mountain can cure a hangover (although it is generally accepted that altitude *increases* the effect of alcohol). But then nothing about this affliction is ever *that* simple.

Folklore has given us a number of hangover remedies that are every bit as curious as George's. In medieval England, for instance, it was said that the folly of drinking too much mead could be countered by putting a mixture of bitter almonds and pieces of raw eel into a person's first drink of the day. More likely to make the unfortunate soul feel he was seeing things than to cure his aching head, I would have thought! A seventeenth-century scientist, Robert Boyle, was, I suspect, drawing on an old tradition when he wrote down his *After-Drinking Cure for the*

Heid-ake, which advised: 'Take green Hemlock that is tender, and put it in your Socks, so that it may lie thinly between them and the Soles of your Feet: shift the Herbs once a Day.'

The Native Americans have an equally strange belief that placing some grated horseradish on the forehead and binding this tightly to the head will cure a drink-induced headache. If this doesn't work, the process can apparently be speeded up by placing your thumb in your mouth and pressing it firmly against the roof! In New York in the 1890s, I understand, habitual sufferers looked for relief by allowing themselves to be *leeched*! Although leeches are said to be normally teetotal, there are selected kinds which can become addicted to drink, and it was these who apparently sucked away happily at their relieved patients until falling off stupefied.

In Europe, it was a widespread tradition that moss cultivated inside a skull would cure the pains brought about by too much drinking. The moss had to be dried and powdered and then sniffed up the nostrils for the sought-after relief. An old piece of European witchcraft lore spelled out an even more bizarre remedy. A nail had to be driven into a little wax effigy of someone the sufferer did not like.

How to transfer your hangover.

This was supposed to transfer the hangover to the unsuspecting victim. Now haven't we all wished on occasions that our hangovers belonged to *someone else*?

The Chinese, an altogether more sensible people about such things, have for centuries recommended chewing a raw root of ginger or eating some spring rolls as a curative. The Dutch prefer a bowl of sheep's feet, cow's livers and oatmeal which has been boiled for six hours before being strained and eaten hot. The ever-practical Germans maintain that a dish of sauerkraut and sausages, or else three soused herrings with a small glass of Pils, are the answer to an aching head.

In Ireland, it is not a piece of blarney when they suggest half-a-dozen oysters washed down by a pint of Guinness. Apart from the pleasure in supping this remedy, the oysters apparently contain zinc which is good for a body whose own supplies of the mineral have been seriously depleted by alcohol. The Australians believe that a greasy hamburger or 'pie floater' (meat pie) coated with tomato ketchup and swallowed with a large glass of iced tomato juice will do the trick! And, finally, in Puerto Rico I'm told they use lemons or limes as a curative because of the astringent properties of the two fruits. It's not that which surprises me. Just the fact that you are supposed to rub the slice of lemon or lime *into your armpits*!

Some of these ideas are rather less than scientific, of course, and what is really called for is a more practical approach to the state of emergency in which the hangover sufferer finds himself. Or, to use the correct terminology for it, 'a nutritionally self-induced type of cerebral malfunction'. But we won't let big words confuse the issue.

Basically, it seems to me, hangovers come in three types:

1 *The Monster Maker.* The all-consuming type which greets you with a massively throbbing head, a feeling of nausea in your stomach, and the certain knowledge that if you open your eyes the world will turn over and you will be violently sick. This, more than the other two, is the inspirer of those immortal lines, 'I *swear* I'll never touch another drop again!'

2 *The Time Traveller.* This hangover is far less overwhelming than the *Monster* and puts you in a trancelike state in which your mind seems

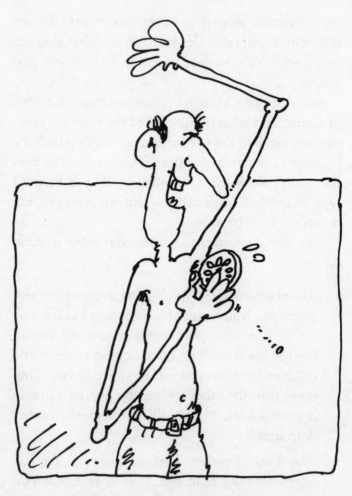

The Puerto Rican hangover cure.

detached from your body and all you need is to be left alone in stillness and silence. Especially the latter—for with this type even the sound of a butterfly walking across the window can be excruciating. The *Traveller* inspired the well-known phrase, 'My head feels as if it is floating.'

3 *The Slow Burner.* Guaranteed to catch out the unwary. The hangover that isn't—until you go about your business. Then the conviction that you have survived unscathed from last night's drinking is rudely upset by an outbreak of sweating, a headache and a desperate need to find a loo. It often produces the cheery remark from others, 'You *look* how I feel!'

Having established which type of hangover you are suffering from, there are three ways of tackling it:

1 **Pretend it is not there.** Clearly impractical as well as painful and unpleasant for you and anyone who has the misfortune to cross your path— husband, wife, mistress, boss or whoever. (You'll probably want to stay well clear of the friends who got you into this state in the first place.)

2   **Disguise the fact.** This is often a necessity
    when the wheels of commerce must continue to
    grind even if you have a set of your own already
    hard at work inside your head. A couple of
    tablets containing paracetamol are probably the
    best emergency action, followed by a swig of
    mouthwash to disguise the alcohol fumes you
    are emitting like a blow torch, and a pair of
    dark glasses for those watery, bloodshot eyes.
    (The reason for their vampire-like amber glow is
    because the alcohol has been busy on its nefari-
    ous mission expanding your blood vessels. This
    has caused more blood to flow through the
    vessels and consequently those nearest the sur-
    face of the eyes become more noticeably red.)

3   **Face up to it.** You're a big boy (or girl) and
    there is only one thing to do with a hangover:
    get rid of it. Which is the reason why you've
    bought this book (or borrowed it, shame on you:
    think of the poor author's royalties!) in order to
    become privy to my methods of feeding and/or
    drinking it into submission. For there are, in fact,
    two alternatives—with a combination of both
    being perhaps the most efficacious of all.

We'll take the liquid solutions first and then move
on to food, leaving to the last those weird and won-
derful concoctions known as 'a hair of the dog'.

Because dehydration is the root of the problem it
must be tackled first. If you have not taken Sir
Kingsley Amis's advice and got those bottles of
mineral water waiting for you and your thirst when
you wake, there is no alternative but to get up.
Which is rather a pity, because tiredness and lack of
sleep may well be part of the reason why you've got
a hangover and there are lots of people who argue
that the only recipe for the morning after is *rest*. So
another forty winks would be beneficial.

But if needs must—and especially if the protests
from your brain and stomach are becoming ever
more urgent—then it is time to rise and face the day.

A pint of ordinary water or mineral water is the
ideal first step towards recovery. Or better still, water
with a pinch of salt and a teaspoonful of sugar dissolved in it. The reason for this is that your body
contains a balance of minerals like sodium, potassium, calcium and magnesium. Dehydration can
upset their balance, pushing them into storage areas,
and one way to correct this and ensure a return to
normal service is with treated water.

It is probably worth re-emphasising here that most hangovers only cause mild dehydration and water on its own is probably quite sufficient in the majority of cases. There is, however, a medicine called Dioralyte available at chemists for treating a severe case of dehydration—but this does not contain any ingredients to numb the hangover headache.

Now, as the intake of water starts to bring relief to the parched terrain that was previously your stomach, follow this up with a cup of coffee, with or without milk. If you prefer, have a glass of milk on its own (milk and yoghourt are both reckoned to be good absorbers). Some doctors recommend soft drinks such as orange squash or lemonade as another way to combat the dehydration; others feel that unsweetened fruit juices or grapefruit can play an equally useful part.

Behind this advice lies the fact that while the alcohol was swooshing through the body it took away vitamins like B1, B6 and C, which have to be replaced. So fruit juice and vitamins B and C come highly recommended. A Nobel prizewinner, Dr Linus Pauling, has even claimed that vitamin C is not only good as a hangover remedy, but when given quickly in large doses—between five and 30 g—it can sober up someone who is completely drunk in a matter of minutes rather than hours. Some Scots, I am told, claim that a fizzy orange-coloured drink native to their land, called Irn Bru, has almost mystical powers in putting their lives back into focus.

A pint of apple juice has a lot to be said for it, too—so long as it is one of the plain, unsweetened types. It is claimed to be cleansing to the palate as well as a laxative and diuretic to the other parts of the body.

By now you should be sufficiently recovered to think about taking some solids on board. The well-tested theory about this stage of the hangover cure goes like this. Your stomach is still partly asleep—may even be a little paralysed from all the alcohol that has gone through it—so what it needs is something easily digestible that will kick-start the gastric juices into flowing once again.

A bowl of milky cereal or a yoghourt are ideal for the sensitive tum in which alcohol has been busy making acid all night long like some personal illicit still. The irritated walls particularly are in need of some TLC. Bread soaked in milk and eaten like porridge can help this; while chicken soup contains all the right ingredients, but may just *not* be what you fancy first thing in the morning! Bananas are also good for the battered brain cells—like all the fruit sugars, or fructose—because they can provide energy and also help stabilise the liver.

Opinions seem to be polarised about the great British breakfast of eggs and bacon. Some health experts argue that however much you may crave a big fry-up, it is the worst thing to dump on a delicate stomach. Others believe that because it is important when tackling a hangover to increase the depleted blood sugar level in the body, a protein-rich breakfast including a plentiful helping of carbohydrates can build up the sugar and energy levels. And what fits this criterion? Eggs and bacon (for proteins) and toast and marmalade (the carbohydrates). As someone who enjoys a fried breakfast whatever misdemeanours occurred the night before (well, *most* times), I can only suggest that the reader and his stomach make up their own minds on this one.

Among other starter dishes which have been recommended to me, four are from authorities whose reliability is beyond question. The late Scottish novelist Alistair MacLean swore by grilled kippers soaked in the juice of a whole lemon (the combination of an oily fish and the lemon to speed up the production of alkalis in the stomach). The great French wine expert André Simon stood by his countrymen's recipe of raw herrings, onions and sour cream; while TV chef Keith Floyd suggests a bowl of cockles sprinkled with white pepper and eaten with sliced white bread and butter. Another media personality, Clement Freud, has his own recipe for what he calls 'Hangover Casserole'. To make it, he says, thinly slice half a kilo of onions, simmer them in a saucepan with half a pound of butter until soft, and then pour in a bottle of champagne. Next, decant the mixture into a soup tureen, cover with a layer of Camembert cheese and sprinkle on toasted breadcrumbs. The 'casserole' should then be baked in a medium oven until the cheese has melted and the crumbs have become crisp. 'Eat it for breakfast,' advises Freud, 'after seasoning with black pepper.'

If you have the stomach for making *that*, you probably don't have a real hangover at all! (Those who can't face all the preparation might like to try an easy alternative, also with champagne, which I am told French wine growers offer to hungover guests: a mixture of one part cognac to three of fizz.)

Athletes who have celebrated a victory just a little too enthusiastically have come to the conclusion that exercise is the best remedy for a hangover. They greet the new day confident in the knowledge that fresh air and running (or swimming) will help sweat out the toxins. For those used to vigorous exercise, this is probably a good idea psychologically as well as physically, because exercise can take the mind off the rest of the body's problems. But it is not a solution to be recommended if you don't work out regularly, in which case it will probably only further enrage your overloaded system.

Two alternatives to exercise are a sauna or a massage. The heat of the sauna is good for sweating acids and alkalis out of the body, while aromatherapy is gaining new adherents for much the same reason. Evening primrose oil, too, has been employed successfully in massage, thanks to a substance in it which can change the types of prostaglandins our bodies produce. These are a range of chemicals active in the body which influence the way we feel pain and thus help in getting the aches and pains of a hangover under control. (On these same 'open-the-pores' principles I have even been recommended to shovel down a really hot curry—

but then my informant *was* of Indian birth!)

One kind of exercise that is recommended for everyone is a good wash and brush-up. A hot shower or bath is ideal for getting rid of that grubby feeling which invariably accompanies the morning after—but *not* a cold one, despite what any macho friend may say. (Ask *him* to show the way if he insists on its therapeutic value.) Washing the hair is another good idea, and has the psychological value of taking your mind off your suffering. A wet shave can also work wonders. (Men only, of course.)

Our forebears used to direct some of their attention to their tongues. Indeed, in Georgian times, gentlemen would set about their hangovers with a quick glass of hock-and-seltzer and then start scraping off the coating of fur that made swallowing such a trial. The special 'tongue scrapers' they used, made of silver with turned ivory handles, are now very collectable and can occasionally be bought from antique dealers. I think I'll stick to scraping my beard rather than my tongue, thanks!

That guru of the morning after, Sir Kingsley Amis, is the proponent of what I believe is the most unusual and potentially most enjoyable cure of all— *if* you are up to it. Let me quote from his book *On*

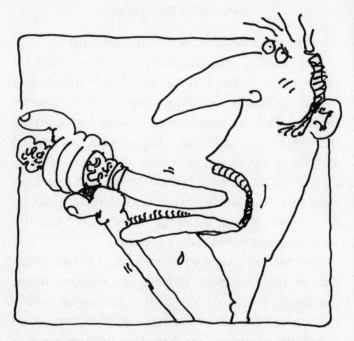

Georgian tongue scrapers are now very collectable.

Drink (1972), in which he writes about waking up: 'If your wife or other partner is beside you, and (of course) is willing, perform the sexual act as vigorously as you can. The exercise will do you good, and—on the assumption that you enjoy sex— you will feel toned up emotionally.'

Amis does, though, add a word of warning: '(1) If you are in bed with somebody you should not be in bed with, and have *in the least degree* a bad conscience about this, abstain. Guilt and shame are prominent constituents of the Metaphysical Hangover, and will certainly be sharpened by indulgence on such an occasion. (2) For the same generic reason, do not take the matter into your own hands if you awake by yourself.'

Thinking about sex—and not in a smutty way or in my cups—I always get a smile from one useless piece of information that 'men and women expend as much energy in a single act of sex as is required to stand at a pub bar or cocktail party and chat for eight hours.' Now who on earth worked *that* out!

If you happen to be on your own, however, then deep breathing and controlled relaxation of the body are not a bad idea. Extra oxygen helps the metabolism of alcohol and relaxation settles a restless mind. It is my belief that this should be part of your overall cure once the worst symptoms of stomach upset and headache are disappearing. Sitting comfortably *upright* (note this) take slow, deep breaths—about one every six seconds. Then consciously relax the different parts of your body, starting with the face and neck, moving through your arms and chest and down through the thighs and legs to your feet. A number of drinking acquaintances of mine use this method regularly and claim that it relaxes the whole body wonderfully and at the same time seems to remove all the feelings of anxiety and tension which accompany a hangover. A more vigorous alternative is to go for a walk, breathing in while taking five strides, holding your breath for another five, and then exhaling slowly as you walk five more. After five minutes, the effect can be quite amazing.

Before the invention of aspirin by the firm of Bayer, Meister & Lucius in the early years of this century, a lot of people tried to cope with their hangovers by putting a bag of ice on their heads and their feet in a bowl of hot water. This was supposed to 'take the blood from the brain' and relieve a throbbing head. Today there are still people who claim this method can bring a sense of relief, although few actually use the ice bag or hot water. The bag has now been replaced by a packet of frozen peas—though it is as well not to leave it on your poor suffering cranium too long in case it thaws, the bag splits and the soggy mass only adds to a complexion that is already green!

The manufacturing of hangover cures has now become big business, with firms all over the world producing a whole range of pharmaceutical products that make billions every year. Some of these are headache removers, others are indigestion relievers, and a small group offer a combination of both pain-killer and antacid. Five brands in the latter category have been singled out for me by grateful users and I pass on their recommendations.

The best-known of these 'answers to the morning after' is *Alka-Seltzer*, which contains aspirin, citric acid and sodium. It is the combination of the sodium bicarbonate and citric acid which partly protects the stomach as well as producing the familiar 'fizzing' when water is added. *Andrews Answer* is a mixture of paracetamol, caffeine and sodium bicarbonate in which the caffeine acts as a mild stimulant and raiser of spirits. *Beecham Resolve* contains paracetamol, citric acid, sodium bicarbonate, potassium bicarbonate, sodium carbonate and vitamin C. The extra ingredient of vitamin C is the added attraction of this brand. *Boots Headache and Indigestion Relief* is a mix of paracetamol, caffeine, citric acid, sodium bi-carbonate and sodium carbonate in which, again, the caffeine is intended to give a 'lift'. *Superdrug*

Paracetamol Seltzer combines just paracetamol and sodium bicarbonate, which are probably the two most important ingredients of a hangover cure.

Again, trial and experience will probably decide which, if any, of these proprietary brands suit your brand of headache because, of course, different products can affect different people in different ways.

There is also a small group of products known as 'pick-me-ups' which I would be failing in my duty—and in the interests of your hangover—not to mention. Many years ago, herbs were acknowledged to be useful in setting the system right, as the following description of an eighteenth-century 'surfeit-water', which contained no less than 21 different varieties, makes delightfully clear:

> It is used successfully against cholicks, gripings in the stomach and bowels, flatulencies and vapours, all of which it discusses by its carminative virtue. It attenuates the humours, and helps perspiration, and is therefore good in all epidemical and contagious distempers. It resists putrefaction and expels the malignity from the centre to the circumference, which it discharges by a gentle dew upon the surface of the cuticle.

Today, the best known pick-me-ups are un-doubtedly *Fernet Branca* and *Underberg* which are part and parcel of any good barman's equipment and not a bad thing to have in the cupboard at home, either. *Fernet Branca*, in its distinctive bottle which has been manufactured in Milan for more than 150 years, is a 'bitters liqueur' containing extracts of over forty selected herbs including angelica, bryonia, camomile, myrrh and saffron, all mixed in alcohol to a secret formula with a proof of almost 80 per cent. *Underberg*, on the other hand, is called a 'herbal digestif' and is made in Germany from a selection of herbs from 43 different countries with alcohol. It is less bitter in taste than its rival, but slightly more alcoholic (84 per cent proof). Although neither manufacturer claims that they are hangover cures, both liquids undoubtedly get the gastric juices moving and restore a sense of well-being.

Less well-known is D. R. Harris & Co.'s *Original Pick-Me-Up*, containing alcohol and other ingredients, including camphor and chloroform, which the company has been making for over 200 years. The *Pick-Me-Up* has long been popular in high society and is said to be recommended by the Queen Mother.

In solid form you can take your choice between *Milk Thistle*, *Nux Vom* or *Berocca* tablets. *Milk Thistle* or *Silybum marianum* (and I'm not making that up) has been available the longest, the Ancient Romans having first spotted its curative properties. The large prickly plant with red flowers from which the extract is taken originated in Kashmir, where growers crush the stems to obtain a milky white juice. This is made into tablets which, when swallowed, work in the liver, barring the throughflow of toxins and also stimulating the production of protein. Despite its somewhat unsettling name, *Nux Vom* is a homœopathic remedy to clear the head and settle the stomach, aimed at those who like to combine New Age attitudes with old world drinking bashes. Lastly, *Berocca*, which I first encountered in Australia where it originated. These are tablets of vitamins B and C, and they fizz violently when dropped into water. Although not claimed to be a hangover cure, they are highly recommended by some Aussie boozers as the perfect nightcap to prevent a 'bonzer splitty'.

In 1993, an announcement from an American pharmaceutical company, CompuMed, seemed to herald the arrival of every drinker's prayer—the cure to end all cures, the remedy to clear up even the worst hangover in minutes rather than hours. The name of this elixir was SoberGain. The makers said that it worked by lining the intestine with extra supplies of the enzymes that break down alcohol. It would, said CompuMed, have the double strength of being able to prevent drunkenness if taken before a bash, and sober up a victim in double time in the morning. Three years later, I'm sorry to have to say that SoberGain has not yet been marketed, although I'm told the research is going on. You don't think they could be keeping a good thing to themselves, do you?

And so to the hair of that infernal dog as the final resort of the hungover. Some people hold firm to the idea on the grounds that as the body is dehydrated it can help relieve the symptoms because it adds liquid. Others deny this, claiming that, as alcohol is a sedative, all it can possibly do is abate the hangover temporarily. A further group warn that any so-called remedy consisting of alcohol which is taken first thing in the morning has to be the first step towards alcoholism. Neither I nor my publisher (and we both like a drink, thank you very much) are prepared to take sides in this argument. Those who want to drink should be allowed to drink—the only question seems to be the amount. And *that* is a personal matter.

The remedies which I have collected from a whole cross-section of people and sources all over the world follow in the next chapter. They range from the efficacious to the unlikely, and although all have been carefully researched and a number actually tried by family and friends, they come with no guarantee. In fact there is, as yet, no surefire, cast-iron, solid gold way to cure a hangover other than time. Only—as I have tried to show in the preceding pages—how to make the morning after feel better.

You are therefore invited to continue to the next page entirely at your own risk . . .

FIVE

HAIR OF THE DOG
A Vade-mecum of Remedies

There are two quite distinct schools of thought
about the 'hair of the dog': those who think it works
and those who don't. But the sheer number and
variety of these remedies long ago convinced me
there was more than a little *something* for the hangover in the idea. Precisely *what* is only to be discovered by trying.

Although the distinguished wine expert Cyril Ray
did not really subscribe to the view that taking
something nasty must be doing you good, he did
admit that 'they must all be based on some sort of
sympathetic magic, on the principle of strong devils
driving out weaker devils.' Timothy Coffee, the
editor of the *Journal on Alcoholic Studies*, puts a
different slant on the argument. He thinks a hangover may be nothing more than your guilt complex

at getting drunk in the first place: 'Come morning, you are going to feel guilty about hanging one on. Guilt feelings about anything can give jitters and aches. So go ahead and concoct some foul-smelling remedy. It's a good way of punishing yourself and thereby relieving the guilt.'

I'm not sure that *I* feel guilty about the occasional bit of overindulgence, but I do believe there is one factor about the 'hair of the dog' principle that is often overlooked. As I hope I've made clear in this book, it is important not to rush the curative process. The brain, in particular, must be allowed to return gradually to its normal activity. Therefore a dash or two of alcohol—the dog that bit in the first place—will allow the brain cells to recover *gently*. The last thing it or your body needs is another shock.

So with the proviso that there is no absolute guarantee given with any of the remedies that follow, make your selection, take your medicine, and *bon chance*!

KEY

SPIRITS
Single measure ..... 25 millilitres   (⅞ fl. oz.)
Double measure ..... 50 millilitres (1¾ fl. oz.)

WINES
Standard glass ......125 millilitres (4⅝ fl. oz.)

Black Velvet

half-bottle of Guinness
extra dry champagne

One of the world's most famous hangover remedies which every Irishman claims as his country's own. Using a half-pint glass, half-fill with Guinness and then top up with the champagne which must be extra dry, according to those of experience. This is a cure to be taken slowly—and it would be a shame to leave the other half . . .

Bloody Mary

single vodka
1 bottle (or can) chilled tomato juice
1 teaspoon Worcester sauce

2 teaspoons lemon juice
Tabasco sauce
rock salt and red pepper

Another very famous remedy, which is now served
in a number of variations although the original
recipe, created by a bartender at Harry's New York
Bar in Paris, specified the ingredients listed above.
It is said to have been named after Queen Mary
Tudor who earned the nickname 'Bloody Mary'
for the enthusiasm with which she executed her
enemies, and the legend has grown of a remark
made in 1954 by Ernest Hemingway when a barman served him the drink to help him disguise from
his wife, Mary, the fact that he had been drinking.
So successfully did it fool Mrs Hemingway that the
delighted writer told his friend behind the bar the
next day, 'We've caught her out—that bloody
Mary!' The most widely used constituents are six
parts of tomato juice (for nourishment) to one part
of vodka. To this add the lemon juice, Worcester
sauce, dash of Tabasco and a sprinkling of salt and
pepper. Stir vigorously, adding a little crushed ice.
Swallow quickly.

Bloody Pint

half pint bitter beer
half pint tomato juice

The less famous remedy which is said to have originated in Manchester. A pint glass is half-filled with tomato juice and the bitter added. This cure is sometimes also referred to as 'Foaming Blood'.

Bullshot

double vodka
small tin beef consommé
1 lemon
1 teaspoon Worcester sauce
1 teaspoon Tabasco sauce
1 teaspoon horseradish sauce
1 egg
rock salt and red pepper

Apparently invented during the early days of the transatlantic liners, the 'Bullshot' is recommended as a substitute for breakfast. First put two handfuls of crushed ice into a jug and add the consommé, the squeezed juice of the lemon, the shot of vodka, and the sauces. Stir the mixture until it is smooth and then pour out sufficient to fill half a glass. To this carefully add the yolk of a fresh egg and sprinkle with salt and pepper. Drink the yolk at one swallow. The 'Bullshot' can alternatively be made with a tin of V8 vegetable juice and very dry gin in place of the vodka. The Tabasco and horseradish sauces are omitted and the whole mixture is strained into a tumbler. The egg yolk is similarly optional.

California Sunrise

1½ measures rye whiskey
champagne
absinthe
Angostura Bitters
½ teaspoon sugar

A popular remedy in Hollywood, believed to have been first concocted in a Sunset Boulevard hotel for a well-known female silent movie star, to sober her up for the studios. Using a whisky tumbler, mix a dash of Angostura Bitters with half a teaspoon of sugar. To this add the rye whiskey, an ice cube, and top up the glass with cold champagne. Before drinking, add two dashes of absinthe (see also 'Sydney Sunrise').

Captain Blood

Bundaberg rum
small measure lime juice
Angostura Bitters

An Australian favourite, although it takes its name from the popular character in English fiction, the pirate Captain Blood, created by Rafael Sabatini, who also wrote the classic historical romance, *The Tavern Knight* (1904). The remedy should be made in a tumbler with four measures of the rum, a shot of lime juice and two dashes of Angostura. According to regular users, the Captain is best taken neat, although ice can be added to help it down a parched throat.

Champagne Charlie's Cure-all

half bottle champagne
1 teaspoon cognac
Angostura Bitters

A favourite with hungover Victorian revellers which was offered in many fashionable London hotels as a precursor to the first meal of the day. The champagne must be ice cold and served in a large, chilled glass. Add the cognac and a dash of Angostura Bitters, stir vigorously and drink rapidly.

The Chairman's Ticket

large port
small brandy
1 egg
sugar

Believed to be the invention of a buffet car attendant on a London-bound train in the Thirties, for the benefit of some of his hungover city gentlemen. After mixing the port and brandy, stir in an egg yolk and half a teaspoon of sugar. 'The Chairman's Ticket' is best drunk slowly, making allowances for the swaying of the carriages.

Cider Pick-up

single apple brandy
single Dubonnet
Angostura Bitters

The good folk of the West Country have been making cider for centuries—and hangovers are no mystery to them. One traditional remedy claims that just two tablespoons of cider vinegar (*not* ordinary cider) on their own will lift a bad head in no time. The 'Cider Pick-up' is a more recent concoction and calls for the apple brandy and Dubonnet to be stirred into a large glass of ice, adding a dash of the Angostura, and then strained before drinking. When pronounced in the West Country dialect this cure sounds like 'Cider Picker'.

The Corpse Reviver

brandy
Fernet Branca
white crème de menthe

The invention of this hangover cure is credited to London's famous Savoy Hotel in the Strand, which has played host to many important guests from the worlds of politics, entertainment and sport. 'The Corpse Reviver' is made up of one third of brandy to a third of Fernet Branca and the same of white crème de menthe—the measures depending on the severity of the hangover!—then shaken with ice and served in a cocktail glass.

The Farmer's Friend

double vodka
milk
2 Alka-Seltzers
tomato juice
Worcester sauce

Variations of this remedy are to be found all over the world—especially in Russia where it may well have originated. The milk is an important part of the cure and ideally should be warm from the cow. (Fresh full-cream milk can be used as a substitute.) To half a glass of this add the vodka, the two Alka-Seltzers, 50 millilitres of tomato juice and a dash of Worcester sauce. Stir vigorously until the mixture has a foamy appearance. Drink slowly.

The Flippant Hen

light ale
1 egg

The hangover recipe that bell boys the length and breadth of America used to recommend to hungover guests—especially because it was so quickly and easily made. To a small bottle of beer add one whole egg, then shake and stir. Drink quickly while handing over tip.

Gaslight Tiger

Dubonnet
Pernod
bourbon
lemon

The Tiger has for years been a night club favourite in the United States among seducers, because it apparently has aphrodisiac qualities. It is important first to rinse a glass with Pernod and then add ice cubes, followed by one part of Dubonnet and three parts bourbon. The mixture should be stirred vigorously and garnished with a twist of lemon. If being offered to a woman, 'The Gaslight Tiger' should be accompanied by lots of flattery.

Guy Fawkes' Explosion

brandy
vermouth
Pernod

A story, certainly apocryphal, says that this mixture

A cure to be treated with the utmost caution.

was devised by Guy Fawkes for drinking after one late night session with his fellow conspirators. The three types of liquor have to be mixed in equal parts and stirred well before serving. A mixture consisting of a third of a bottle of each is said to be enough to explode half-a-dozen hangovers. To be treated with the utmost caution!

Hair of the Dog

single whisky
1 tablespoon double cream
1 tablespoon honey

This archetypal hangover remedy, which has been served to uncounted millions of sufferers all over the world, is best made in a cocktail shaker with plenty of ice, the noise of the ice cubes being the prelude to blessed relief. To the scotch, add the cream and honey and shake vigorously. 'Hair of the Dog' is best drunk in a cocktail glass held with both hands!

Hangman's Blood

champagne
double whisky

double gin
double rum
double port
double brandy
bottle of stout

One of the most fearsome of all hangover cures, which was recommended by the author Anthony Burgess as his favourite eye-opener. The aptly named drink is made in a pint glass into which are poured the large measures of whisky, gin, rum, port and brandy, followed by half a pint of stout. The glass is then topped up with champagne. 'Hangman's Blood' has a smooth and very heady taste and a pint of it is certainly enough for two hangovers if you have a friend in the same condition!

Hart's Starter

brandy
2 garlic cloves

Not to be confused with the famous 'Heart Starter' (see below), this curative was created and patented by Nathan Hart in England in 1904. It actually has to be made *before* hanging one on. Pour a bottle of brandy into a saucepan and mix in two chopped up cloves of garlic. This unappetising brew must then be slowly heated for an hour, rebottled, and kept in a warm place for at least a week to ferment before it is ready to use. A double measure should suffice for the brave of heart.

Heart Starter

double gin
Andrews liver salts
water

Renowned as one of the quickest and easiest remedies to make. To the double gin add a teaspoon of Andrews liver salts and water. As soon as the fizzing has abated, swallow the 'Heart Starter' in one gulp.

Highland Fling

1 pint buttermilk
1 tablespoon cornflour
salt and pepper

An ancient, non-alcoholic Scottish recipe which is claimed to be particularly good for whisky-generated hangovers. Heat the buttermilk—which ideally should be fresh from the churning—stirring in the cornflour until the mixture almost reaches boiling point. Add a pinch of salt and pepper and drink as hot as possible.

Horse's Neck

double scotch
ginger ale
lemon

A great favourite in the Navy after a heavy night in the wardroom. Peel the whole rind of the lemon and place this in a tall glass spiralling up from the bottom with the end hanging over the top. Add two cubes of ice, pour in a large whisky and fill with cold ginger ale. A dash of Angostura Bitters is optional. 'Horse's Neck' can be equally effective when made with brandy.

The Hot Pope

tokay
ripe bitter orange
sugar
nutmeg
cloves

Named after the lusty Pope John XII who revelled in party-giving and apparently used this mixture to revive himself on grey Vatican mornings. Heat half a pint of the sweet and aromatic Hungarian wine almost to boiling point, and pour this over the oranges in a heat-resistant tumbler. Mix in the sugar, nutmeg and cloves to taste and drink slowly.

Jamaica Sunrise

single Jamaica rum
1 teaspoon liquid honey
1 teaspoon cream

Famous throughout the West Indies, this remedy combines three delicious ingredients to relieve a hangover as gently as the waves that lap the shores of that tropical paradise. The rum—a strong proof is recommended—should be shaken with ice and the other two ingredients before being strained into a glass. Drink in a shady spot.

Jules' Remedy

Pimms No. 1
grand marnier
champagne

Named after the famous Jules Bar in Jermyn Street, London, where the barmen make it better than anywhere else! To the Pimms No. 1 add a small measure of grand marnier and fill up the rest of the glass with cold champagne. There are few more pleasant ways to ease a throbbing head!

Khan's Curse

1 teaspoon cream of tartar
1 teaspoon Epsom salts
1 teaspoon ground ginger

Although Genghis Khan was a man who loved a drink—and probably suffered a hangover or two—there is no reason for the name of this non-alcoholic remedy beyond its use of tartar. The three ingredients should be mixed together in a glass and then dissolved with water. Swallow quickly to relieve your head of the curse!

Milk of Human Kindness

double cognac
half pint fresh milk
Angostura Bitters
sugar

A popular remedy with the farming community, this cure has been made in one variety or another for the past two centuries. In East Anglia for many years the cognac was provided by smugglers bringing it in from France to grateful customers. Add the spirit to the milk and shake well with ice before topping off with a teaspoonful of sugar and a dash of Angostura. 'The Milk of Human Kindness' is best drunk in a tall glass; and some of its devotees claim that a squirt of soda water gives the remedy an added zest.

Morning Glory

double whisky
small absinthe
1 egg
2 teaspoons sugar syrup
lime and lemon

The preferred remedy of a lot of wine and spirit merchants. Best made in a shaker, first adding the whisky and absinthe to crushed ice. Follow this with the syrup, *white* of the egg (note: *not* the yolk) and the juices from half a lime and half a lemon. It should be strained into a tall glass and topped up with an equal amount of soda water. Another hangover cure, also known as 'Morning Glory', consists of just a large measure of Fernet Branca and a dash of peppermint, which has to be swallowed in one gulp.

Mr Pepys' Breakfast

1 pint strong ale
1 glass red wine
1 glass white wine
1 dozen oysters
1 ox tongue
6 anchovies

The famous diarist Samuel Pepys, whose patron was the Earl of Sandwich, was a prodigious eater, drinker and womaniser, as his diaries, originally written in cipher, have revealed. In an entry for New Year's Day, 1661, he gives the ingredients for a remedy he said he regularly served to friends suffering from hangovers, which consisted of: 'A barrel of oysters, a dish of neat's (cow's) tongues, a dish of anchovies, wine of all sorts and North-downe Ale.'

New Orleans Eye-opener

champagne
cayenne pepper

Recommended by the famous Brennans Restaurant in New Orleans, one of the must-visit places in the French Quarter, as the way to start the day when you are suffering from the effects of the night before. The suggested amount of champagne is usually a half-litre, each glass being sprinkled with the famous pepper which originated from the city of that name in French Guiana. Buttermilk is sometimes mixed with the champagne in equal quantities for lady guests. Cayenne is also used in another remedy which includes a glass of milk and two tablespoons of castor oil. While heating the milk and oil, sprinkle on the pepper and allow the mixture to become lukewarm. It should be sipped slowly.

The Peter the Great

double brandy
pepper

This remedy was devised by the Russian emperor, Peter I, known as the Great, who introduced changes in dress, manners and etiquette in his capital, St Petersburg—not to mention protracted drinking bouts. The brandy must first be warmed, liberally spiced with pepper and then drunk at one swallow.

Polish Bison

double vodka
teaspoon of Bovril
2 tablespoons lemon juice
pepper

Sir Kingsley Amis, of whom I need say no more if you have been paying attention throughout this book, is credited with inventing the awesome 'Polish Bison'. Pour at least a double vodka into a glass and add a large teaspoon of Bovril beef extract plus two tablespoons of lemon juice. Stir this vigorously, adding a little water and pepper, and swallow as quickly as possible.

Prairie Oyster

single cognac
1 teaspoon wine vinegar
1 teaspoon tomato ketchup
1 teaspoon Worcester sauce
cayenne pepper
egg yolk

Believed to have originated in the old Wild West of America, although today the making of a 'Prairie Oyster' is an essential skill for any bartender worth his salt in any part of the world. With the exception of the egg yolk and the cayenne pepper, mix all the ingredients together in a small tumbler. Add the pepper and then drop in the yolk without breaking. Drink down in one, swallowing the egg whole. According to popular lore, this cure was named after the appearance of the egg yolk staring up at the drinker attempting to swallow it in one! Some British barmen use a tablespoon measure of the vinegar, ketchup and Worcester sauce, and add Angostura Bitters to the ingredients.

Rhumba Tummy

vinegar
ground quassia

This non-alcoholic remedy has been popular in South America for over a century and utilises the bitter-tasting bark and wood of an indigenous local tree, the *Quassia amara*, which has been used even longer as a tonic and cure for fever. The cure suggests using a pint of strong vinegar with an ounce of finely ground quassia. This should be allowed to ferment in a bottle for at least a day before being used. The ideal way of taking 'Rhumba Tummy' is two teaspoonfuls in a small glass of water.

Rum Nog

4 tablespoons rum
4 tablespoons cream
1 tablespoon sugar
1 egg
nutmeg

Just one of the many famous 'nog' varieties. First mix 2 tablespoons of rum with the egg yolk and sugar, and allow to stand for an hour. Then beat the egg white until it is stiff, stir into the yolk and rum mixture and add the remainder of the rum. A 'Rum Nog' looks at its most inviting when a little nutmeg is sprinkled on the top. This tasty cure can be made in exactly the same way with scotch, brandy or bourbon.

Scots Wha Ha'e

double whisky
small Pernod
Fernet Branca
Tabasco
salt

A favourite with Scottish golfers facing the rigours of an early morning round with a late-night hangover on board. This is one remedy that has to be mixed gently. Add the Pernod to the whisky, followed by the dashes of Fernet Branca and Tabasco. A couple of ice cubes and a pinch of salt should be added while stirring—then strain the mixture into a tall glass and savour every mouthful.

Sea Captain's Special

double rye whiskey
champagne
absinthe
sugar
Angostura Bitters

Created in a waterfront bar in San Francisco by bartender Harry Porter, for seamen hungover after a night of carousing. The first ingredient is a lump of sugar doused in Angostura. Put this in a tall glass, adding the double measure of rye and topping off with champagne. The *pièce de resistance* is the two dashes of absinthe. Highly recommended by US Navy sailors, this drink is admiringly known as 'distilled dynamite'.

Singapore Sling

double gin
small cherry brandy
ginger ale
Angostura Bitters
lemon or lime juice

It is said that this drink was originally concocted in

the famous Raffles Hotel in Singapore and, true or not, it is certainly of oriental origin. Mix the gin and cherry brandy, adding the juice of a quarter of a lemon (or alternatively a large lime) plus a dash of Angostura. When well shaken, the mixture should be strained into a tall glass. Add an ice cube and top up with ginger ale. Some barmen recommend topping off the Sling with a slice of lemon peel which can be sucked between mouthfuls.

Sputnik

large vodka
Fernet Branca
1 teaspoon fresh lemon
1 teaspoon sugar

According to popular legend, the 'Sputnik' is said to have been created in 1961 by disappointed (and hungover) American space scientists in the immediate aftermath of the launching of the pioneer Russian space craft. The vodka should be mixed with an ounce of Fernet Branca to which the sugar is added and stirred until dissolved. Then add the lemon juice and some ice cubes. Strain the mixture and drink slowly to ensure a safe return from orbit.

Suffering Bastard

large brandy
large gin
lime juice
ginger ale
Angostura Bitters

Another famous remedy which has been attributed to a barman working in the old Shepheard's Hotel in Cairo just prior to World War Two. The brandy and gin are poured into a glass, followed by a double measure of lime juice. Top up with ginger ale and a dash of Angostura Bitters. This is one cure that should be sipped *slowly*! The Americans have a similar version known as the 'Dying Bastard', in which a double bourbon is added to the ingredients.

Sydney Sunrise

fresh orange juice
1 lime
1 dessertspoonful liquid honey
1 egg
nutmeg

Another in the 'Sunrise' series, this one comes recommended by the English TV chef Keith Floyd. The 'Sydney Sunrise' should be made in a blender into which is put the squeezed juice of a lime, the honey, yolk of an egg and half a pint of orange juice. Activate the blender until the ingredients are thoroughly mixed and then pour the drink into a glass containing several ice cubes. Sprinkle on freshly grated nutmeg and sip slowly.

Tiger's Milk

double cognac
double Bacardi
half cup cream
half cup milk
nutmeg

This is an authentic Thai hangover cure which has recently been introduced to the West thanks to the increasing number of Thai restaurants. The remedy is best made in a shaker with plenty of ice, pouring in the ingredients as listed above. When mixed, 'Tiger's Milk' should be sprinkled with a little nutmeg before drinking.

Virgin Mary

1 bottle (or can) tomato juice
1 lemon
celery

No one has claimed the invention of this non-alcoholic remedy, although a slightly malicious rumour has suggested it was developed by some libidinous French monks in one of the famous wine-growing regions! The tomato juice is mixed with the lemon juice and a finely diced stick of celery. A pinch of pepper and salt should be added before drinking.

The Evelyn Waugh

champagne
lump sugar
Angostura Bitters
red pepper

Evelyn Waugh, the great imbiber and author of such classics of social drinking and dining as *Vile Bodies* (1930) and *Brideshead Revisited* (1945), developed this hangover cure which bears his name. First soak a lump of sugar in Angostura and roll it in red pepper. Slip this gently into a glass of champagne and then watch for a moment as each bubble of fizz carries a grain of pepper up to the surface ready for the palate. It is a remedy, in Waugh's own words, that is 'painfully delicious'.

White Shoulders

double vodka
single curaçao
1 oz (25 g) double cream

A creation of the Jazz Age in America, 'White Shoulders' was devised as a pick-me-up for hungover flappers as the dawn came up. The vodka and curaçao should be mixed in a large glass with ice cubes, and the cream added last. Shake the mix thoroughly and strain before serving.

Yellow Fever

juice of 2 lemons
1 teaspoon mustard

This last remedy, I am told, originated in South Australia where it is sometimes referred to as the 'Pommy Hot Dog'. The mustard powder should be mixed thoroughly with the squeezed lemon juice and taken in one swallow. It is *hot*!

SIX

THREE SHEETS TO THE WIND
The Wit and Wisdom of Drinking

THE DRINKER'S MOTTO
The man who has never been drunk does not know the value of sobriety.

Chinese aphorism

THE SECRET OF THE BOTTLE
Oh, that second bottle, it is the sincerest, wisest, and most impartial down-right friend we have; tells the truth, of ourselves, and forces us to speak truth of others; sets us above the mean policy of Court-Prudence, which makes us lie to each other all day, for fear of being betrayed by each other all night.

John Wilmot, Earl of Rochester, *Works* (1926)

AN ABSURDITY

To get drunk—and complain the next morning of a headache.

George Manville Fenn, *Absurdities* (1896)

THIRST OF THE DAY

Of seeming arms to make a short essay,
Then hasten to be drunk, the business of the day.

John Dryden, *Epilogue to Constantine the Great*
(1667)

NO STOMACH FOR IT

Many a man keeps on drinking till he hasn't a coat to either his back or his stomach.

George D. Prentice (1865)

THE DAY AFTER

Let us have wine and women, mirth and laughter,
Sermons and soda-water the day after.

Lord Byron, *Hours of Idleness* (1807)

THE ANAESTHESIA OF LIFE

Alcohol is the anaesthesia by which we endure the operation of life.

George Bernard Shaw (1928)

TOAST FOR THE DAY

I feel sorry for people who don't drink. When they wake up in the morning that's as good as they are going to feel all day long.

Dean Martin (1966)

LOCKED OUT

A giddy young fellow of Sparta,
To hangovers had long been a martyr,
    Till his wife, so they say,
    Took his latchkey away,
He was smart, but the lady was smarter.

Anonymous (1933)

HAIR OF THE DOG

Take the haire, it is well written,
Of the dog by which you've been bitten
Work off one wine by his brother
One labour with another.

Antiphanes (479 BC)

LOOKING FOR SUPPORT

A witness being interrogated in a London court about whether the defendant in a case was still hungover from a drinking session the previous night, replied, 'Well, I can't say that exactly; but I saw him sitting in the middle of the floor of his room, making grabs in the air, and saying that he'd be buggered if he didn't catch the bed the next time it ran around him.'

Anonymous, *Wit and Humour* (1979)

PUSSY-FOOTING

I was left in no doubt as to the severity of the hangover when a cat stamped into the room.

P. G. Wodehouse (1936)

THE LOST FORTNIGHT

I went on a diet, swore off drinking and heavy eating, and in fourteen days I lost two weeks.

Joe E. Lewis (1939)

ON PRESCRIPTION

I reminded him of that old saying, 'There are more old drunkards than old doctors.'

J. P. McEvoy (1968)

'I was left in no doubt of the severity of the hangover . . .'

RUB IT AWAY

Animal Henry sat reading *The Times Literary
Supplement,*
with a large Jameson & worse hangover.
Who will his demon lover
today become, he queried. Having made a dent
in the world, he insisted on special treatment,
massage at all hours.

John Berryman, *Recovery* (1973)

SMITTEN BY REMORSE

The next morning the moment when I awoke, O
mercy! I did feel like a very Wretch. I got up, &
immediately wrote & sent off by a Porter, a Letter
—I dare affirm, an affecting & eloquent Letter to
him—& since then have been working for him, for I
was heart-smitten with the recollection, that I had
said all, all in the presence of his *Wife.* He admitted
that altho' he never to the very least suspected that I
was tipsy, yet he saw clearly that something unusual
ailed me. What a woman to instigate him to quarrel
with *Me*!

Samuel Taylor Coleridge, *Letter*
(20 February, 1804)

NO ESCAPE

And then . . . you know how if you've had a few
You'll wake at dawn, all healthy, like sea breezes,
Raring to go, and thinking: 'Clever you!
You've got away with it.' And then, oh Jesus,
It hits you.

James Fenton, *The Memory of War* (1983)

FILL HIM UP AGAIN!

Sunday, 26 September. I awaked at noon, with a severe head-ache. I was much vexed that I should have been guilty of such a riot, and afraid of a reproof from Dr Johnson. I thought it very inconsistent with that conduct which I ought to maintain, while the companion of the Rambler. About one he came into my room, and accosted me, 'What, drunk yet?'—His tone of voice was not that of severe upbraiding; so I was relieved a little.—'Sir, (said I) they kept me up.' He answered, 'No, you kept them up, you drunken dog.' This he said with good-humoured English pleasantry. Soon afterwards, Corrichatachin, Col and other friends assembled round my bed. Corri had a brandy-bottle and glass with him, and insisted I should take a dram.—'Ay,' said

Dr Johnson, 'fill him drunk again. Do it in the morning, that we may laugh at him all day. It is a poor thing for a fellow to get drunk at night, and skulk in bed, and let his friends have no sport.'

James Boswell, *The Journal of the Tour of the Hebrides*
(1785)

BITTER CURE

Well, tomorrow perhaps I'll drink beer only. There's nothing like beer to straighten you out, and a little more strychnine, and then the next day just beer—I'm sure no one will object if I drink beer. This Mexican stuff is particularly full of vitamins, I gather . . .

Malcolm Lowry, *Under The Volcano* (1967)

THE PRICE OF GIVING IT UP

I felt my heart curl and my scalp hum. Why? I gave up spirits three days ago. Giving up spirits is okay so long as you drink an incredible amount of beer, sherry, wine and port and can cope with especially bad hangovers. I think I had an especially bad hangover.

Martin Amis, *Money* (1984)

AN ADMIRABLE CORRECTIVE

My own preference is for nothing more magical or esoteric than the patent medicine, Alka-Seltzer, that admirable corrective for gluttony and alcoholic remorse. Take no notice of the namby-pamby instructions on the bottle about one or two tablets being the adult dose, but put four in a tumbler of water, the colder the better—a lump of ice does not come amiss—and let any genteel inhibitions about belching go with the wind.

But I cock a wary eye at those hardened sinners who lace the Alka-Seltzer with a large gin. True, I have seen a chemist writing somewhere that it is ridiculous to suppose that anything will cure a hangover, and that the effect of effervescent alkalis is purely psychological. So, very often, is a hangover: if I should *seem* to have a hangover, I should be quite pleased to have it *seem* to be cured.

Cyril Ray, *Ray on Wine* (1979)

NEVER MIX

I should never have switched from Scotch to Martini.

Humphrey Bogart, last words (1957)

REMORSE

The water wagon is the place for me;
At twelve o'clock I felt immense,
Today I favour total abstinence,
My eyes are bleared and red and hot,
I ought to eat but I cannot,
It is no time for mirth and laughter,
The cold grey dawn of the morning after.

George Ade, *The Sultan of Sulu* (1904)

HEROIC DRINKER

The best thing I have done is drink . . . I have written much less than most people who write, but I have drunk much more than most people who drink.

Guy Debord's epitaph (1994)

THE CREATIVE URGE

It was the only good writing I ever did directly from a drug, even if I paid for it with a hangover beyond measure.

Norman Mailer, *Advertisements for Myself* (1959)

MYTHS

The history of Europe can be considered as the history of myths; over and again political movements owe their power to the propagation of the undesirable legend. But the use of myths has a similar effect to the use of alcohol: an inevitable hangover follows the original elation.

V. S. Pritchett, *New Statesman* (July 1942)

THE COFFEE CURE
Coffee started as a medicine; its ability to quicken the spirits, and, above all, to remove the vestiges of those severe hangovers which afflicted our hard-drinking forefathers, soon brought it into wide use.

Aytoun Ellis, *The History of Coffee Houses* (1957)

THE FINAL STRAW
There is no cure for the hangover, save death.

Robert Benchley (1952)

CLOUDY FORECAST
A drunken night makes a cloudy morning.

T. Fuller, *Gnomologia* (1732)

GAUDY MORNING
'Serves you right,' said Harriet to Miss Cattermole who opened her eyes with a groan. 'If you must take your drink like a man, the least you can do is to carry

it like a gentleman. It's a great thing to know your own limitations.'

Dorothy L. Sayers, *Gaudy Night* (1935)

IN THE COLD GREY DAWN

There was a young fellow named Vaughan,
Who got terribly drunk on caughan.
    In the cold grey daughan,
    Of the following maughan,
He wished he had never been baughan.

Anonymous, *Smart Set* (1932)

SOBER AGAIN

A little learning is a dang'rous thing;
Drink deep, or taste not the Pierian spring:
There shallow draughts intoxicate the brain,
And drinking largely sobers us again.

Alexander Pope, *An Essay on Criticism* (1711)

DOWN THE DRAIN

His lordship had drunk his bath and gone to bed again.

Anonymous (c. 1928)

NOTHING NEW

I felt a bit hang-overish, but that was nothing new.
Patrick Quentin, *Puzzle for Fools* (1936)

MAKING SENSE

I reminded him how heartily he and I used to drink
wine together, when we were first acquainted; and
how I used to have a head-ache after sitting up with
him. He did not like to have this recalled, or perhaps
thinking that I boasted improperly, resolved to have
a witty stroke at me: 'Nay, Sir, it was not the *wine*
that made your head ache, but the *sense* that I put
into it!'

James Boswell, *Life of Johnson* (1791)

HANGING ID ON

I do not think that anyone completely understands
its mechanism, but it is a fact that there are for-
eign substances which, when present in the blood
or tissues, directly cause us pleasurable sensations;
and they also so alter the conditions governing our
sensibility that we become incapable of receiving
unpleasurable impulses.

Sigmund Freud, *Civilisation and Its Discontents* (1937)

THE GREEN LIGHT
Last evening you were drinking deep,
So now your head aches. Go to sleep.
Take some boiled cabbage when you wake
And there's an end of your head ache.

Athenaeus, *Banquet of the Learned* (c. AD 200)

ALL'S NOT WELL
All was pretty well till I got to bed, when I became
somewhat swollen and considerably vertiginous. I got
out and, mixing some soda-powders, drank them off.
This brought on temporary relief. I returned to bed;
but grew sick and sorry once again. Took more soda-
water. At last I fell into a dreary sleep. Woke, and was
ill all day, till I had galloped a few miles.

Lord Byron, *Journals* (1816)

THE CRAPULA TRAP
The drunkard now supinely snores,
His load of ale sweats through his pores,
Yet when he awakes the swine shall find,
A crapula remains behind.

Charles Cotton, *Burlesque upon Burlesque* (1930)

THE REAL THING

This was a hangover. The real thing. Thank god he was dressed, he wouldn't have the dressing to go through, the fumbling with buttons, the insoluble puzzle that would be the shoelaces.

Charles Jackson, *The Lost Weekend* (1944)

A CURING DRAUGHT

3 April. Up among my workmen—my head akeing all day from last night's debauch. To the office all the morning; and at noon dined with Sir W. Batten and Pen, who would needs have me drink two good draughts of Sack today, to cure me of last night's disease—which I thought strange, but I think find it true.

Samuel Pepys, *Diary* (1661)

THE PORTER'S PROVOCATIONS

MacDuff: What three things does drink especially provoke?
Porter: Marry, sir, nose-painting, sleep and urine. Lechery, sir, it provokes and unprovokes: it provokes the desire but it takes away the performance. Therefore much drink may be said to be an equivocator with lechery: it makes him and mars him; it

sets him on and takes him off; it persuades him and disheartens him; makes him stand to and not stand to: in conclusion, equivocates him in sleep, and, giving him the lie, leaves him.

MacDuff: I believe drink gave thee the lie last night.

Porter: That it did, sir, i' the very throat on me; but I requited him for his lie, and, I think, being too strong for him though he took up my legs sometime, yet I made a shift to cast him.

William Shakespeare, *Macbeth* (1605–6)

THE CURSE OF NEW WINE

And how did Noah react when he awoke with one of those knifing new-wine hangovers? He cursed the son who found him and decreed that all Ham's children should become servants to the family of the two brothers who had entered his room arse-first.

Julian Barnes, *A History of the World in 10½ Chapters* (1989)

HAIR OF THE MASTIFF

He said, 'I kept trying to get up, and every time I took my head off the pillow, it would roll under the bed. This isn't my head I've got on now. I think this is something that used to belong to Walt

Whitman. Oh dear, oh dear, oh dear.'

'Do you think maybe a drink would make you feel better?' she said.

'The hair of the mastiff that bit me?' he said. 'Oh, no, thank you. Please never speak of anything like that again. I'm through. I'm all, all through.'

Dorothy Parker, *The Penguin Dorothy Parker* (1973)

THE INCOMPARABLE REMEDY

Indian tonic-waters had been proposed to me by an aged lay-brother as an incomparable specific for the thirst.

Flann O'Brien, *At Swim-Two-Birds* (1939)

THE HORRORS OF PENITENCE

Amid the horrors of penitence, regret, remorse, head-ache, nausea, and all the rest of the hounds of hell that beset a poor wretch who has been guilty of the sin of drunkenness—Can you speak peace to a troubled soul? My wife scolds me! My business torments me! And my sins come staring me in the face, every one telling the more bitter tale than his fellow.

Robert Burns, *Letter to Robert Ainslie* (1791)

THE TISSUE-RESTORER

He returned with the tissue-restorer. I loosed it down the hatch, and after undergoing the passing discomfort, unavoidable when you drink Jeeves' patent morning revivers, of having the top of the skull fly up to the ceiling and the eyes shoot out of their sockets and rebound from the opposite wall like racquet balls, felt better. It would have been overstating it to say that even now Bertram was back again in mid-season form, but I had at least slid into the convalescent class and was equal to a spot of conversation.

P. G. Wodehouse, *The Code of the Woosters* (1938)

THE UNANSWERABLE QUESTION

Never ask me why. I don't know the answer. If I did, I wouldn't do it.

William Faulkner, *Knight's Gambit* (1950)

'Never ask me why . . .'

BIBLIOGRAPHY

The following are a few of the works I consulted during the writing of this book. I need hardly draw the reader's attention to the curious titles of some of the books, nor the even curiouser names of some of the authors!

Blue, Frederick O. *When A State Goes Dry*, American Issue Publishing Company, 1916.

Blunier, O. *The Barkeeper's Golden Book*, Mortgarten-Verlag, 1935.

Blythe, Samuel G. *Cutting It Out: How to Get on the Waterwagon and Stay There*, Forbes & Co., 1912.

Cherrington, Ernest Hurst. *History of the Anti-Saloon League*, Anti-Saloon League, 1913.

Clarke, Eddie. *Shaking in the Sixties*, Cocktail Books Ltd, 1966.

Druit, Robert. *Report on Cheap Wine*, Henry Renshaw, 1865.

French, Richard Valpy. *Nineteen Centuries of Drinking in England*, Longman, Green & Co., 1884.

Grindrod, Ralph Barnes. *Bacchus: An Essay on the Nature, Causes, Effects & Cure of Intemperance*, William Brittain, 1848.

Gull, William W. *The Alcohol Question*, Strahan & Co., 1905.

Gutzke, David A. *Protecting the Pub: Brewers and Publicans Against Temperance*, Boydell Press, 1989.

Healy, Maurice. *Stay Me With Flagons*, Michael Joseph, 1940.

Iglehart, Ferdinand Cowle. *King Alcohol Dethroned*, Christian Herald, 1917.

Juniper, William. *The True Drunkard's Delight*, Unicorn Press, 1933.

Mendelsohn, Oscar A. *The Earnest Drinker*, George Allen & Unwin, 1950.

McPhun, W. R. *The Anatomy of Drunkenness*, Robert Macnish, 1834.

Peabody, Francis G. *Substitutes for the Saloon*, Houghton Mifflin, 1901.

Prescott, Henry P. *Strong Drink and Tobacco Smoke*, Macmillan & Co., 1869.

Simon, André. *Bottlescrew Days*, Gerald Duckworth & Co., 1906.

Startling, Ernest H. *The Action of Alcohol on Man*, Longman, Green & Co., 1923.

Terrington, William. *Cooling Cups & Dainty Drinks*, George Routledge, 1869.

Trader Vic. *Bartender's Guide*, Garden City Books, 1948.

Wilson, Charles. *The Pathology of Drunkenness: A View of the Operation of Ardent Spirits*, Adam & Charles Black, 1855.

ACKNOWLEDGEMENTS

I must extend my special thanks for their help in the research for this book—above and beyond the call for another round and the consequences thereof—to the following hearty imbibers: John Kent, George Farrow, Doug Impett, Mike Tew, Peter Eden, Richard Morris, Cliff Baker, Richard Haining, Jonathan Waring, Tom Gondris, Hugh Phillips, Ross Duke, Nigel Hawkes, Jane MacQuitty, Nicki Pope and the anonymous long-suffering soul who prefers to be remembered as Uncle Tom Cobblers. Also my publisher, Ernest Hecht, who kept me guessing for twenty questions (which I failed to get right) over dinner before commissioning this book. It's been one headache I've enjoyed.

Thanks also to the following authors and their publishers for permission to quote from their inestimable books on the follies of drinking: Hutchinson Publishing Group for *On Drink* by Kingsley Amis and *The Code of the Woosters* by P. G. Wodehouse; J. M. Dent for *Ray on Wine* by Cyril Ray; Faber for *Recovery* by John Berryman; Penguin Books for *The Memory of War* by James Fenton, *Civilisation and its Discontents* by Sigmund Freud, *The Lost Weekend* by Charles Jackson, *The Penguin Dorothy Parker* by Dorothy Parker and *Knight's Gambit* by William Faulkner; Jonathan Cape for *Under the Volcano* by Malcolm Lowry, *Money* by Martin Amis, *Advertisements for Myself* by Norman Mailer and *A History of the World in 10½ Chapters* by Julian Barnes; Victor Gollancz Ltd for *Gaudy Night* by Dorothy L. Sayers and *Puzzle for Fools* by Patrick Quentin; and lastly Methuen Publishers for *At Swim-Two-Birds* by Flann O'Brien whose comic genius would drown any hangover.

A.T.

**More books for imbibers
from Souvenir Press**

YOUR GOOD HEALTH!

The Medicinal Benefits of Wine Drinking

Dr E. Maury

How to cure ailments and disorders by drinking particular wines whose special properties can alleviate the problem—Champagne *brut* for indigestion, Médoc for heart conditions, Chablis for kidney function.

HARRY'S ABC OF MIXING COCKTAILS

Harry MacElhone

with new material by Andrew and Duncan MacElhone

The cocktail-maker's bible, by the proprietors of Harry's New York Bar in Paris, the oldest cocktail bar in Europe. Presented alphabetically with a thumb index—everything from the 'Abyssinia Cocktail' to the 'XYZ', with advice on mixing and serving cocktails the professional way.

THE ILLUSTRATED WINESPEAK

and

SOMETHING IN THE CELLAR

Ronald Searle

Laugh away your hangover with these two hilarious wine books with a difference—from a master cartoonist in full colour.